THE SHIP OF BIRTH

Also by Greg Delanty

POETRY

Cast in the Fire
Southward
American Wake
The Hellbox
The Blind Stitch
Collected Poems, 1986–2006

SPECIAL EDITIONS

The Fifth Province
Striped Ink

TRANSLATIONS

Aristophanes, *The Suits* (originally titled *The Knights*)
Euripides, *Orestes*
The Selected Poems of Kyriakos Charalambides
The Selected Poems of Seán Ó Ríordáin

EDITED VOLUMES

Jumping Off Shadows, Selected Contemporary Irish Poets (with Nuala
    Ní Dhomhnaill)
The Selected Poems of Patrick Galvin (with Robert Welch)

THE SHIP OF BIRTH

POEMS

GREG DELANTY

LOUISIANA STATE UNIVERSITY PRESS

Baton Rouge

Published by Louisiana State University Press
Copyright © 2007 by Greg Delanty
All rights reserved
Manufactured in the United States of America
First printing

Designer: Laura Roubique Gleason
Typeface: Janson Text
Printer and binder: Edwards Brothers, Inc.

LIBRARY OF CONGRESS CATALOGING-IN-PUBLICATION DATA

Delanty, Greg, 1958–
  The ship of birth : poems / Greg Delanty.
    p. cm.
  "An earlier and somewhat different edition of this book was published in Britain
and Ireland from the Oxford poets series of Carcanet Press (2003)"—T.p. verso.
  ISBN-13: 978-0-8071-3218-0 (alk. paper)
  ISBN-13: 978-0-8071-3219-7 (pbk. : alk. paper)
  1. Childbirth—Poetry. I. Title.

PR6054.E397S55 2007
821'.914—dc22

A number of the poems in this collection first appeared in the following journals:
*Agenda, American Scholar, De Brakke Hond, Contemporary Poetry of New England,
Foilsiu, Fulcrum, Helicon, Metre, Natural Bridge, OnEarth, Partisan Review, Poetry
Daily, Poetry Ireland Review, Poetry Review, The Recorder, Salt, The Shop, Southern
Review, Southword, Times Literary Supplement, TriQuarterly.*

An earlier and somewhat different edition of this book was published in Britain
and Ireland from the Oxford *Poets* series of Carcanet Press (2003).

For Daniel especially

Lie still in thy berth
and I'll log the days
of your arrival—may
my words
be lanugo-soft
for fear
they turn you
away.

Five major worldwide extinction events have struck at biodiversity since the origin of complex animal life some 535 million years ago. Global climate change and other causes, probably including collisions between the Earth and extraterrestrial objects, were responsible for the main extinctions of the past. Right now we are in the midst of the sixth extinction, this time caused solely by humanity's transformation of the ecological landscape.

Engraved matter-of-factly on the floor of The American Museum of Natural History, New York City

CONTENTS

THE SHIP OF BIRTH

THE ALIEN

I'm back again scrutinizing the Milky Way
    of your ultrasound, scanning the dark
        matter, the nothingness, that now the heads say
    is chockablock with quarks & squarks,
gravitons & gravitini, photons & photinos. Our sprout,

who art there inside the spacecraft
    of your Ma, the time capsule of this printout,
        hurling & whirling towards us, it's all daft
    on this earth. Our alien who art in the heavens,
our Martian, our little green man, we're anxious

to make contact, to ask divers questions
    about the heavendom you hail from, to discuss
        the whole shebang of the beginning&end,
    the pre–big bang untime before you forget the why
and lie of thy first place. And, our friend,

to say Welcome, that we mean no harm, we'd die
    for you even, that we pray you're not here
        to subdue us, that we'd put away
    our ray guns, missiles, attitude and share
our world with you, little big head, if only you stay.

PAPER LIGHT

Today's light would break the hearts of the dead
       if they could step back in.
The sun filters through the lightest haze, a gauze
       of light
swabbing eye-cataracts that shroud what must be
       spirit-eyes.

It's as if the sun is seen through Japanese rice paper
       laid over
a timeless print or poem, suggesting core light
       that the sketch
or calligraphy leaves out, so the essence blazes
       through
—what the ghosts might call the divine, that may
       be seen only at one remove.

Or, as now, at one remove through this haze's tracing
       paper, the kind that as kids we simply
traced the sun, clouds, water, trees, people, cars
       and boats of our crayon-colorful world through.
As it is now and never again shall be: fawn-fall grass,
       the milkweed-seeded air, the vermilion trees,
the lake's veiled boats, the ghost of a passing truck
       and the gray scribble
on this paper white as a wimple, lit up as if from
       inside
by the unseen grand hand on this day that breaks
       the heart of a man gone all simple.

ACCORDING TO THE NEPALESE

The kith and kin souls of those who've gone hover
      above the couple making love, elbow into
the woman's underworld, drinking the man's buttermilk
        in their ghostly death-drought, to recast our ilk.
Welcome Mona, olla Anna Lopes Ferreira, and you
      Rob, and all the Danny Boys. I could go on forever
invoking the dead. Each clamouring chromosome
      roll-calls out of the past, at home
        in this character small enough to set down
      within the palm of my hand. Our dust-come-to-life,
whose antique eyes have you? Whose frown?
      Whose disposition? Whose strain of strife?
We toast you now, our ancient child risen from the tomb,
kidnapped by a band of ghosts, bound in your dark room.

MORNING WATCH

The percolator is a gurgling alembic
       brewing the morning's spluttering slick.
I bask in the coffee's simple balm.
           For once I'll be wise and forgo
           turning to the company of the radio,
           the world's hourly news, and see
           if the goldfinch and the chickadee
              will come to our feeder,
         to our coffee-brown sunflower seed.
I'll accept the responsibility of being calm.
I'll pay attention to the small creatures,
       to their broadcast and morning need.
       This morning I will pay special heed.

SONOGRAM

Now it's like a flashlight fanned down into the dark
              you've landed in,

not unlike a cross section of the light wedge
revealing the missing child after the toddler
              wandered off from the picnic
              and the ground opened up
                 burying him alive
                 in the escape vault
             of an abandoned mine.

Each parent faults the other.
               *
When the doctor points to a white hole,
    the screen's bright nebula,
and matter-of-factly mouths words
    we can't understand,
except for "*possible* chromosome abnormality,"
    I thought of the drinking night
    about the time we gave up hitting the jackpot
of you, our mite.
Next day I heard your mother sigh
    in the guesthouse bathroom
        as the EPT popsicle stick
        turned a stop-light red.

The doctor's words
        recalled the hangover pallor
          of her face.
They settle in her stomach like lead.
              *
Our newfound mummy in a crypt,
  —so fragile that even a mere gust
        must turn you to dust—
I knock on wood for you
        in your birth box.
May we only have to welcome you
    into the school of normal hard knocks.

SOUND KINETICS

It dawned on me as we woke to Manhattan's sea-sound
          of traffic, how this is akin to what you hear,
pressed like an ear to the shell of your mother,
          unable to match sound to moving bodies.

I could tell you, since the doctors say you can
          distinguish voices and we must converse with you,
that the scraping of a steel ladder telescoping up
          the walls outside our window, heavenward,

is secure, and that the window cleaner
          works our window into an angel's sudsy wings
before he whistles to the top story and climbs off
          to loll away the day on cloud nine;

that the hammering is a cavil playfully
          demanding everyone on the street be quiet
to allow the sidewalk magician to saw
          a street volunteer in half; or

that the soft moans of a woman and man
          is a couple making out. These are, of course,
all hypotheses, conjectures of sound;
          tall noise without a hint

of the window cleaner's drudgery,
          the carpenter's impatience, the traffic
that is more a tinnitus than a calming susurrus,
          and, a white lie for another reason entirely,

that the moaning—which, by the way,
          has stopped now—was a couple next door
and not, of course, your Ma and Da. This is no more
          than an exposé on the kinetics of love.

SIGHTINGS

All week I've been out of kilter, down in the dumps
        for no apparent reason.
Perhaps, I've simply been too balanced, happy even,
        and the roller coaster
god of humour, doctor Mood-Swinger himself, has said
        "Enough.
You're gettin' under my skin. Old boy, it's time for
        your general depression shot."
                        *
Now it's midmorning and I still can't get going. I potter
        round the house
and say alright, so be it, welcome Mr. Down, Mr. Nightday,
        old faithful companion.
                        *
No sooner did I shake hands with Squire Black and we get
        all chummy, inseparable even,
than this pair of goldfinch perch on either side
        of our pendulum feeder.
One's the yellowest yellow I have ever laid eyes on,
        the other's an off-yellow.
They are my selves: the upbird and the off-yellow
        downbird, balancing the fulcrum. I look up.
The birds take off out of sight into the summer-thick air.
        Soon enough I'll be out of here myself
soon enough. That's alright now though.
        That's alright.

THE EXPECTED

You've been lying low, keeping mum
of late. On coveted nights, our chum,
your mother and I have forgotten
you're there, settling into our routine,
on the lam from quotidian strife:
money worries, the brandished knife
in the email, the hell-for-leather
workaday world, the lousy weather.
Perhaps you've sensed what lurks outside
and decided simply to hide
the way creatures do before a storm,
their antennae sensing harm.
Have you picked up how we're slow
to relinquish the world that we forgo
to have you, our sulking mouse? You see,
your mother and I are not unhappy
alone together. Do you understand?
Many a day we are grand,
simply chatting with one another,
spoofing away bother.
Chitmouse, it's impossible to explain
our lives before your reign.
It's as if we're quietly dying
and know it, wondering
at our terminal time, coveting the last
haven weeks as they trimester past.
But for your sake I'll say no more.
Mum's the word now, a stór.

THE AIR DISPLAY

Squadrons of geese fall-fly south, moving in
      and out of rank,
honking simply to stay together and to swap
      leader.
The teachers urge the children to look at fighter
      jets, the Thunderbirds,
a name taken from the great Indian bird, but
      nothing is said of that provenance.
The new god rips open the tepee vault of the sky
      above our schools and homes.
No one points out the caret of geese inserting
      themselves peacefully on the day,
or mentions what exactly the Thunderbirds
      mean to insert.
The geese unravel their chevron ranks, their echelon
      formation and, as if in civil disobedience,
reform again, but this time into a child's copybook
      correct sign.

THE GREAT SHIP

        Later tonight
it's to turn cold, the old sudden sharp
        iceberg cold of New England.
Crickets, cicadas, grasshoppers and frogs
        play on.
What their song and wing-music are saying
        I can't say,
except they must know already that the ice
        has gashed a gaping hole
in the hull of Indian summer, and they
        are the quartet
that comes out on deck and plays away
        as the great ship goes down.
We listen quietly from our deck's lifeboat.
        Play on
brave, noble souls. Play on. *Nearer, my God,*
        to thee. Nearer to thee.

APOLOGY TO CRICKETS

When the squadrons of night-dropped parachutists
       on D-Day were scattered far and wide
       across the occupied French countryside,
finding themselves suddenly alone in forests,
       swamps and fields swarming with the Hun,
they had these thingamajig hand crickets,
       clickers you get in Christmas stockings.
Searching in the dark to hook up with their own,
       they'd cricket-code clickclack clickclack
hearing a rustle of movement, footsteps approaching,
       waiting for the answering cricket greeting.
Tonight, little cricket, unable to hack
       news of another war, I came out to our garden
       and had nothing, nothing to cricket-call you back.

A NEW GENRE

On our deck a dying cricket, a soul
      according to the Algonquin, plays at Fall's end.
They'd say he's the spirit to become you, child,
that he's preparing to vault through your mother
          and enter your body via the manhole
      of your soft-in-the-head fontanelle,
that the cricket's wing-scraping is
your spirit-birth song. Why are there names only
      for death music, death lays?
All day you've been dancing mad in your Ma.
Now I'll take a leap of faith and declare
      the cricket's dying spiritus, his elegy and requiem,
      are your spirit about to enter your corporeal self.
Call this your prelegy and your birthquiem.

THE SEA HORSE FAMILY

The sea horse is a question-mark in the ark of the ocean
      that's carried it without question all this way.
Mythical as a unicorn, and even less believable
      with its dragon head, its body a legless horse
          perpetually rearing, its monkey tail
      anchoring it to sea grass, sponge or coral,
but, my mate,
      no stranger than who you are to yourself,
      feeling large as a whale and small as a human.
Today I'd have us become sea horses, and I,
      being the male, would be the one in the family way.
I'd lug our hippocampus, our *capall mara*, our shy sea pony,
      our question-mark anchored in you,
unquestionably unfurling its self day by tidal day.

THE WORDMEN

It's not impossible that from the very start
      I've been at something akin to
           what the Dogon buckoos do:
how they mussitate extended tales by heart
of the gene-myths of their ancestors into
their women's auricles. And it's these seed-words
           they say—after they enter
      the meatus of the ear and spiral downwards
past the throat and through the proofing liver
      before doing a whirly around the venter
           and settling with a word quiver—
that set the composed woman in the family way.
Incorrect as it is, fantabulous as it sounds, to us,
      it's no more unbelievable, my lovely lay,
than the fetus whorled like an ear in your uterus.

HERO'S RETURN

Most people are caught up in the snow-mobbed day.
       Some are even ecstatic, the snow
            is still, after all, a novelty, a show
                getting under way.
Others are already dismayed,
       cursing impassable streets, traffic delayed
            and the general disarray
of winter giving itself its own ticker tape parade.

THE SHUTTERBUG

The day I developed the negative of a snowflake made by this method and found it good, I felt like falling on my knees and worshipping it.

Wilson "Snowflake" Bentley, Jericho, Vermont, 1885

I want to be a kind of Snowflake Bentley.
After years of standing out in the below zero
weather of Jericho and neighbours declaring him
off the wall, chasing snow chimeras,
he finally caught a crystal and another and
another, invisible white flowers blooming
in the illusory snow desert of winter,
stars whose light has only just become visible,
asterisks footnoting the flaky mystery.
He recalled the Eskimo notion that snowflakes are souls
that descend and enter the expecting mother
and creep into the child's body.
                              And now, our snowdrop,
since your body's all there and the first snow
is falling, softly falling on the world outside
our window, laying out its own carpet
maybe to welcome your soul-star, your soul-flower,
your soul-asterisk into your body
as your mother steps out on the walkway
to fetch the recycling bin. Far-fetched, right enough,
but I peer through our blind as focused
as Snowflake behind his camera's curtain,
a snatcher of snowflakes, to catch
your soul-flake, the forecasted simplicity below
the whole show. I pray, as Bentley prayed
over a fresh crystal, that your flake holds,
that you're not one of those flimsy drops, but rather
a fur-flake, snug and at home as a fur-coated Eskimo
stepping out of your igloo into the universe of snow.

THE SOUL HUNTER

*The Tongons imagined the human soul to be the finer or
more aeriform part of the body . . . something comparable
to the perfume or essence of a flower as related to the more
solid vegetable fiber.*

Edward Burnett Tylor, *Religion in Primitive Culture*, 1958

People have their smells too,
indefinable odors,
individual
as a fingerprint;
how I spirit-whiff
the redolence in homes
beside coffee, dinner, diaper, and other
somatic potpourri odor;

how a girlfriend
has a sweet scent
—a spirit balm
beyond birds' and bees' endorphin beckoners.
She forswears perfume,
costly eau de cologne,
trick-essence that wrists bedaub
to fool other spirits.

The cynic in me smells a rat, this is merely
my human need to sniff out a soul.
Still,
I'll stick to my snout,
hot on the scent of the escaped inmate,
caught from shirt or shoe,
bound to be duped again,
left staring bewildered and foolish

across the scentless bank of the widest of rivers.

SNOW AND WIND CANTICLE TO AN UNBORN CHILD

Now the morning snowstorm is a swarm
of white locusts, not a biblical black wind
devouring all before it, but a charm
of benign creatures whose seeming simple end
is to becalm, dropping a bright humility
on the world, bringing the city to a stand-
still, turning their wings into a white sea
of, when walked on, what sounds like soft sand
that gets piled in snow combers or cotton candy,
or shaped into a button-eyed, carrot-nosed fatso.
Our plump snowman, whose eyes are still as blind
as buttons, soon we'll show you this and so
much more; how now what is called wind
blows a snow kiss, invisible as they say God is.

TO THE BLUE PEOPLE

There's an intangible lazulite blue,
a sheen that glistens off fresh fallen snow,
something akin, but not quite the same as you
see shine off the back of a barn swallow,
the abdomen of a regular bluebottle fly,
the obsidian clear night sky,
the teal of an oil slick, or the halo
of a gas-stove flame—
                                        till visiting Soweto
I realize it is the hint-glint light
shimmering off people unwhite,
finally making sense of why a black man
in Irish is called *an fear gorm*, the blue man.

THE FETAL MONITOR DAY

The Doppler is a metal detector
        combing the hill for treasure
        that the amiable, vigilant nurse
slides over the icy hummock
of your mother's gel-rimed stomach.
           *

Your pounding heart racing toward us
        is the sound of a train at full throttle,
        the tittupping of a galloping horse,
or lovers in the next room of a motel,
the headboard morse-coding against the wall.
           *

Then there's the static of your grand
        kicking like someone tapping
        a mike, testing before the band
breaks into a hit song.
Our star, we're psyched to sing along.
           *

The graph roll of the monitor, a tail
        curling, records the seismic shocks
        of your quakes on the fetal Richter scale,
radiating from the tectonic plate of your Da
rubbing months ago with the hypocenter of your Ma.
           *

You're tucked safely as you can be
        beneath the door jamb of your small room,
        our star, train, love wave, treasure and pony.
Now you've gone quiet as a dormouse,
about to bring down your own house.

THE GOD OF DRY MOUTHS

A storm of tufty snow softly falling is
     white as the God placed on my child tongue,
an O or zero of white, awkward as a kiss,
     set with an Amen, as the choir sang
the Latin canticles, and head bowed,
     hands clasped, I returned to my parents' pew
in my spruce Sunday best, among a hushed loud
     litany of Amens that our God was true
and meek and simple as our set lives were,
     innocent as today's verity of perfect snow
is white. Suddenly, amid shut faces, I'm lost somewhere
     beyond the miscount of seats back to our row.
The host, cleaved to my palate, won't come unclung.
I strain to scrape the dissolving God free with my tongue.

THE PRESENT

Sparrows mostly, but chickadees,
cardinals, finches, wild canaries
feed all day on our birdhouse stairs.
Sunflower seeds, beautiful black tears
your father gave us only a year ago.
He is dead now. How were we to know?
Snow is a white sheet laid silently upon
the body of the earth. How the dead live on.

FOR THE RECORD

Today on Mallet's Bay Avenue I am undone
    by the redivivus of wonder
and not simply by the winter-blade sun
    stirring up the snow's phosphorescence, the under-
iridescence of a pigeon's neck, the jaguar
    in the guise of the svelte street cat.
                              Not simply these,
but the exhaust fuming from a passing car,
    made all the more visible by the freeze
of air, the cumulus of stacks of smoke
    billowing heavenward from McNeil's Generator
and the passing jet drawing a line of coke
    behind it on the sky's blue counter.

Yes, these are not breath or cloud or anything
    to be high on; they undo our skies:
the car we drive, the coffee pot plugged in each morning
    and so on and so forth, but it's nothing but lies
not to reiterate how we, the gallinaceous
    species, can fly, and make invisible flame,
and draw horseless, elephantless, assless luxurious
    cars and trucks. Give us our due all the same
and so forth and so on: how we somehow manage mostly
    to live together—confused only by ourselves, our ghostly
genes of fear and survival, too quick to be undone
    by our invention—mad simply to be under the sun.

THE THIRD TRIMESTER

Child, I'm reduced to playing the amateur masseur,
     quietly desperate, dropping to my knees
to tie your mother's shoes, an obedient chauffeur,
     a bag-lugging coolie eager to ease
your puffed Ma as you blow her up like a balloon
     from the inside—yourself within the zeppelin,
dirigible, hot air, gasbag and rocketoon—
     without ever taking a breath, squashing
her innards, forcing her heart to faint
     on one side, her bursting bladder to leak
continually, her crushed lungs to pant
     just at a walk, her spine to bow by the week.
Soon you will become your own cone-headed arrow,
bursting your bubble, dropping into our good morrow.

THE TURTLE MOTHER

Your mother is a turtle
stranded on her back,
though with her head
—how distorted, contorted,
discombobulated you have her—
turned the wrong way round,
struggling to get up from bed
or couch, flapping her flippers,
helpless, bewildered, sad,
ancient, determined,
a stranger to herself,
and sometimes somewhat scared
hearing unseen rustlings on the banks
of choked weed, stalking, stalking.
How can a turtle know what dark
predators the day will turn up,
except they are legion? She withdraws
into her shell, your dome and home—
tucked into the thought of you?
Good shell, keep her safe and well.

BLACK SNOW

David points at the two-day snow bunkers along Broadway,
     not the natural jaundiced yellow of melting slush,
but as if a storm of smog-snow had fallen.
     He remarks: "That's what we breathe in every day,"
reminding me of how the nuns described the soul
     as a flake of snow and every trespass soot-darkens
that whiteness of whiteness. Ah, the soul of the world
     is made manifest to us today on Broadway and 82nd,
a fuming black exhausted snow-soul, woebegone
     as a bewildered oil-slick bird unable to fly.
I laugh, not without cynicism and apathetic stoicism, qualities
     necessary these days to survive, or rather, to get by.

THE NEO-NATAL

As the curtain open-sesamed on the glass chests
       of incubators—a dozen or so strewn in the cave
           of natal lights shining above resting neonate—
       I tried not to think of them as the glass-caskets
       of deceased saints or royalty and us a wave
           of mourners surging up for one last peek,
or worse again, as a kind of freak show
       as we huddled to gawk,
        though, for all the concerned talk,
somewhere a voice called "Come up, come up, don't miss
           the smallest babies in the universe."

They reminded me more of an aquarium
       of black molly, angel, kissing, tiger, butterfly fish
           seen in a flashy shop or restaurant
           as the winter haunts
       windows and doors with blowing ghost-veils of snow.
               *
Incubators covered with white linen
       —protecting the inhabitants from the lights' glow—
           are snug, snow-covered, gambrel-roofed homes
           in miniature, like our own right now,

       or like the shading
           laid over the canary's cage to fool the maestro
             it's night and forty winks' time
       —ah, little fledglings, perk up your heads and sing.
               *
The nurse draws closed the curtain.
Each child is a magician
       immersed in a glass water tank.
After a breathtaking pause
       may the curtain be unveiled
           and each one be hailed
in a wave of relieved, silent applause.

THE CORONATION

Your head settles into the pelvic butterfly
      of your Ma. Perhaps it's here the soul penetrates
your potentate's body as you slowly pry
      your way out of your watery, burgeoning state.
You make, at best, a willing but much-pressed
      subject and servant of your loyal queenmother,
what with your tantrums giving her small rest,
      waking her at all hours; and every other
minute ordering her to sit on the throne.
      You've grown large and despotic, a parody
of a mad medieval king who is prone
      to great and unpredictable cruelty,
and who now, if we look at Your Highness upside down,
      wears our unsettled kingdom's Pelvic Crown.

THE SHIP OF BIRTH

For months your crib is docked waiting for you,
      laden with a shower of gifts:
hand-knit boots with suede soles, mounting drifts
         of rompers, bibs, hats and a slew
         of other offerings laid on your ship of birth
with the ark story embroidered all about.

In this berth the creatures have mostly mirth-
      ful faces: the cachinnating chickadees, the stout stoat,
      the grinning elephant trunk-bailing the boat,
      the droll owl, the odd rainbow trout,
      the one-humped camel you might think is pregnant
         on its back, the polar bear yodeling upon
            a melting green berg, the avuncular ant,
not to speak of the circus of unrecorded creatures on
      your kid attire. Is this saying, unbeknownst to us,
that we gather around the baby
      The Great Circus of the Earth:
      the flying hippopotamus,
      the fetus-like manatee, the dork stork,
      the delirious giraffe,
         not just for a sappy laugh,
but to illuminate their dearth
and our sapien dodo-ing as we fish-mouth sorry
sorrysorrysorrysorrysorrysorry?

Our little lambkin, waxwing, luckling,
      all the cordial choir are Noah-calling you now:
the lovelice, the leech of paradise, the how-now-down-cow,
the Forever Gone Bird, the Dolly sheep, the flying
kiwi, the crying with laughter jackass, the pronghorn,
the bristleless porcupine, the schizophrenic platypus,
      the liquorice-black crow, the rhinoceros:
         that ancestor of the unicorn
            with an overgrown thorn-horn.

Listen, the horns, the horns are blowing,
trumpeting you, our dear humacorn,

beckoning you onto the ark
        out of your first watery dark.
"Hurry now, hurry now," baritones the polar bear.
        "Our icebergs are melting out here."
"Quick, quick," the duck sections quack.
        "Darn, darn,"
basso-bleats the goat, stomping time with his hoof
        as the chorus raises the roof:
"All aboard, all aboard, our poor wee bairn."

FROM WOODY'S RESTAURANT, MIDDLEBURY

Today, noon, a young macho friendly waiter and three diners,
     business types—two males, one female—
are in a quandary about the name of the duck paddling
     Otter Creek,
the duck being brown, but too large to be a female mallard.
     They really
want to know, and I'm the human-watcher behind the nook
     of my table,
camouflaged by my stillness and nonchalant plumage.
     They really want to know.
This sighting I record in the back of my *Field Guide to People*.

THE ARRIVAL

Shades of waiting for a train in India,
　　　never knowing when it'll show, the dilemma
of having whiled away all curiosity in the other-
　　　ness of the station: the sacred cow
　　　　　　humpbacked like a dromedary or your mother
back-to-front; the platform beggars who kowtow
　　　to the foreigners as yours truly to the doctor;

the lingo, the delivery room's argot that I strain
　　　to make out; the fear there's no train
even as we hear your distant, unseen express
　　　pistoning towards us through the monsoon rain
　　　　　　of monitor static and your mother's distress.
Child, we complain you're overdue;
　　　we crane to catch a first glimpse of you.

A CIRCUS

I doubt anyone would've blinked if a ringmaster
marched in among us and this blarneying broadcaster
raised a megaphone to his lips, announcing
another highlight of the Greatest Show on Earth
along with the likes of the ball-bouncing,
baby-blubber seals; the hoop-leaping lemurs of mirth;
the tremendous, stupendous fandango of horses;
juggling doctors; funambulist nurses;
and all the farraginous farrago of this Earth,
not excluding me, the whistle-blowing clown,
the huffing and puffing red-faced Bozo father
of fathers, wearing a lugubrious frown,
cracking side-splitting sideshow banter
and flat-footed jokes, a sidekick to your mother.
The whole death-defying show spun out of order
as a drumroll hailed you: the debonair,
highflying, daredevil god of the air,
none other than the Cannonball Kid himself
shot from the dilatory, dilative distaff
opening of your Ma, the human cannon herself,
lit a little over nine months ago by your father.
Your gray jump suit was smeared with bloody gauze
as you landed in the hand-net of nurse and doctor;
the whole show agape in the pause before applause.

TO MY MOTHER

You took a deep breath. It was by what we weren't told
we were told. You sidestepped, big-talked of how cold
the winter was, how there was still a test
to come in. "Everything will turn out for the best,
please God." Not till your grandchild was a month old,
not wanting to spoil his entry into the fold,
did you tell us the cancer'd got you buttonholed,
casual, as if it was just a troublesome guest.
                    It took your breath,
the rampant cell's stranglehold
on your alveoli, the invaded hold
of your spiritus. Your chest
tightened as the child's spirit settled in his breast.
Consoled by his arrival, you prayed it could be controlled,
                    not turn out a breath for a breath.

LATE ENTRY

The white sea of a record storm was just ploughed open;
great snow combers held back either side of the road.
There was the quality of the miraculous about the night,
a crossing over out of danger, a leavetaking
and an arrival. While your Ma zipped the overnight bag,
I swabbed the breaking-waters that could've been spilt tea
on our kitchen floor. I pulled the car round to
the front, helped her in as a hooded figure scavenged
our recycle bin, our poor attempt to save the world.
I wanted to call out, say there's no need to scurry
away, a modern-day leper, but another spasm
of your overdue entry had me behind the wheel
and us off, only to be flagged down on Pearl Street
by a police roadblock. Two streets later a driver
in a blizzard of alcohol barred the way, refused
to allow us pass until his girlfriend implored him.
On making the hospital, the nurse assured us
you'd probably slept through it all: the groaning,
the shopping cart's leper-rattle, the swarming police
brisk in the drama of god-knows-what crime,
the drunk man's swearing and so much I've forgotten
or totally missed in the white-out of your storming.

THE LANGUAGE OF CRYING

We're still learning the language of crying,
its parent-boggling irregular grammar.
Anybody would think you were dying.

Puzzling gerunds beyond the clarifying
syllables of raw hunger's regular yammer.
We're still learning the language of crying.

Diaper-changed we take turns rock-a-bying,
bawling at each other please, please be calmer.
Anybody would think you were dying:

a demented king's yowling, terrifying
soliloquy beyond a royal diaper-rash clamour.
We're still learning the language of crying.

Christ child, such a caterwaul's parent-petrifying,
hardly a put on, you're no shammer.
Anybody would think you were dying.

Is it something you sense? A wordless prophesying?
Surely the future's not teething yet. We stammer.
We're still learning the language of crying.
Anybody would think you were dying.

POSTHALAMION

to a newly married couple

The snow which doth the top of Pindus strew,
Did never whiter shew . . .

   Edmund Spenser, "Prothalamion"

Today the snow takes the shape of the world,
having shimmied and trembled in the air
   all night as you slept snow-curled,
flake-furled into each other without fear
for once, of what befalls outside
   your window as if you yourself inside
made the snow fall out of inner air,
confetti-ing the night in a beneficence
   of swan down, keeping souls from the graveyard,
becoming silence
made visible. And yes, you know it's hard
   on some bird or some poor soul barred outside,
   but for now you two are without a doubt
that the world in the window-shard of your yard
   is bright. The wedding-veil snow,
gossamer-light, in the shape of the shed, car, bobsleigh
and frozen lake, takes the shushed aspect of all you know.
And, looking across the whitened bay,
   you recall some deity
         laying himself down across the waterway,
allowing a brace of mortals to cross over in certain safety.

THE GREEN ROOM

Shades of the green room about this scenario.
You lounge beneath the drip of the chemo,
talking shop with others, some bald, some still blest
with their own mops of hair, making the best
of your body's flaw and a visitor's melodrama.
You slip in and out of your latest part: the nausea,
dry mouth, diarrhea, the poison's impact,
having to go back out and face the next act.
The nurse assures you that you look just fine
even in your wig, that you're eternally twenty-nine.
You perk up, introduce "My son, the poet" to everyone.
A bald lady asks, "Do your poems rhyme like that one—
Fear no more the heat o' the sun—we did in school?
Write us one like that." "Okeydoke," says I, playing the fool.

CHEMOTHERAPY

The I.V. bag hangs from the coat rack
of the stand—the revealed trick
up the sleeve
of the doctor, wizard, white-coated necromancer
who would have you believe
that this bag of what
appears to be no more than water
will save you.

Center stage,
you sit and chat
—what can you do?—
surrounded by relatives. You're invincible as Rasputin,
forecasting the future,
feeding yourself doses of transparent poison,
outmaneuvering your disloyal cells' rampage.

A few more treatments and you're through.
You gag.
The nurse peps
you up with banter.
She clips on a fresh drip bag
bulging above you like a strongman's flexed biceps.

THE ROAD HAZARD

Nothing but the quick fix, the narcotic of the car,
    relieved you and us from your caterwaul,
        an option we've resisted so far.
But tonight, short on the wherewithal
    of energy and sleep, we strapped you into
        the car seat's straitjacket, you waking all
           the neighbors. You were sound by North Avenue.
I got the feeling that the highways
    and byways, in the small hours, streamed with a steady dream
        of rookie parents whispering, second-guessing if it's okay
           to sneak home now; those drivers who seem
    to be alone, telling herself or himself not to keep
glancing back at their cradled road hazard for one last peep,
    and not simply to see if their sleep-depriver is asleep.

FONTANELLE

It wasn't until ruffling the tomentose
    of your dark hair and making a gentle tom-
        tom of your head that I felt it. My hand froze
    on the round, soft membrane of your dome.
I must have looked like doubting Thomas
    tentatively touching the unbelievable hole,
        the terrifying recess,
    withdrawing my hand from your poll,
the cerebrum beneath your skull, beneath everything,
    my eyes touch on: the cup, tea, prayer plant, book,
    trees in the window, the window, the workers painting
    across the road, the paint, the shimmering rook.
Now as your parietal bone shuts tight as a walnut,
    I excuse this as tomfoolery and myself a nut.

THE INK MOTH

*introducing Seamus Heaney at the Katharine Washburn
Translation Memorial*

Remember our path crossed the gloaming fall path
of *Isia Isabella*, the woolly
   bear caterpillar? You called it the furry bear.

The bog brown and black mite
—a wee concertina or bellows—traversed our drive's tarmac
      as sails beyond on the lake luffed,
  white moth wings in cuff-white wave tuft.
Someone unseen and unknown laughed,
  a lovely Lucullan disembodied laugh, breeze-lilted
    around the corner of Lake View Terrace and Berry

as Patti welcomed you, her belly a spinnaker
  swelling with the wind, the zephyr,
    of our miteling fluttering in her.

Such a luculent moment has stayed with me. You predicting
  a boy, vatic as the woolly bear
    forecasting winter.
Both of you were right, the winter being severe,
   though not for us,
  and the boy is a reality of flesh
   and bone as I coax from pupae inklings
        this ink moth.
              *
Somewhere the woolly bear opens.
  To call it the furry bear
   is nearer eye-truth,
a miniature dowager's stole worn
to the opera, or some literary hobnobbing shindig. But where
  is Katharine?
She'd be in her element here.

Her company, like yours, Seamus,
   was the spring touch that released in us
    the woolly bear moth,

the love moth I translate it to here,
   stuttering into the air,
   winging it here and here

             and here.

THE NAMING OF CLOUDS

to Katharine Washburn, 1943–2000

This is the weather you loved most of all,
    a snugness of charcoal cloud with rainfall.
I thought at first altostratus opacus.
      But now I'm sure the cloud
        is nimbostratus,
    it being such a shroud
        on the inscape outside my window.
For anyone today passing through here
    for the first time, they'll not know
        the Adirondacks were laid out over there,
    having vanished in the nimbus air
across the stratus of the lake, just as anyone who
    didn't know you will hardly realize you were here.
Or why we peer through the cloud to wherever you
    have gone, shrouded in nimbostratus Katharinus.

THE JOKER FAMILY

You took such care of your hair.
      Now it comes out in clumps. "Maybe
          my new grandson could spare
               a share"
you joked, Barber Death breathing down your neck.
Always joking we are, keeping something or other in check,
      the Joker Family.

Remember how we'd beg you to open the window
      of our gray, white-topped Ford Anglia? But no,
      a mere hairline window crack of in-rushing air
          would toss your hair.
How we sweltered on those eternal drives to Everywhere:
Ringabella, Redbarn, Castlegregory, Glenbeigh.

"Now look at the scenery while the weather's fine," you'd say,
"We'll stop soon and each have a 99," fixing your hair
      in the rearview mirror in that special way.
Ma, any chance of a bit of air?
              *
Lately, on a drive round the Ring, near Kenmare,
      I risked wisecracking how your wig
is almost as good as your own erstwhile hair,
          itself a look-alike periwig,
and that, at least, we can open the car window.
      How we all laughed—you also.
      How the winds blow.

THE WEST

It's a bit like the rhododendron in Kerry,
flourishing west above the lakes all the way
    to Derrynane, the wilder purple kind, beautiful
in itself, yes, beguiling, overshadowing
    quieter plants, not seeing how the shrub
winds its way around and over the native seedlings
    of ash, oak, holly, hazel, fern,
climbing their backs, suffocating them, shutting out light,
    spreading, spreading, spreading; cutting ancient links
in the great chain: the insects, birds, animals,
    even the rare deer of these parts, barring its gentle way.
Still, we're taken by this purple fantasy,
    forgetting the nightmare beneath the flower,
the monstrous root and stem-tendril arms
    that even when cut back gain ground,
squeezing the life out of undergrowth,
    the under-strata of our shaded wood.

THE WAVE

I slip away
      —never being a morning person, as you say—
leaving you crisp as fresh cornflakes, playing peekaboo
      with Dan. He can't find you.
      You're putting a good face on things. Fair dues.
Even if you don't quite know the test's full news.

A boat is shouldered across the dunes off Lamb's Head
      like a coffin. Where do you go when you're dead?
I'd pester you about that, not much older than Danno.

Already you're making ready.
We watch from above. Your boat bobs insecurely.
Run up the sail. Let me give you a hand. Show.
It's so clear on the horizon today
      and the water so calm beyond the bay.
You head out beyond Bird Island towards Teach Duinn.
      A quick getaway would be a boon.
      Dan has learned to wave now too.
         He'll never remember you.
Look Ma, my hand. You'll be out of sight soon.

TIES

to Harvey Shapiro

I savour your poems on a park bench as Dan sleeps.
Bikers, joggers, skateboarders race to stay youthful.
Aphrodite floats by on rollerblades. A train hoots to a halt,
slowly shunting down the worn ties of last century.
Daniel wakes, wakes me to him. His baby hand grips
the pages of *This World*. The train hoots again and moves on.

SHOPPING FOR A COMPOSTER

Rooting around what simply looked like refuse bins
I sounded out the petite clerk. Opening an exhibit,
she picked up a rotting fruit to expose worms
covering the flesh. She talked of them naturally,
endearingly even. I'll try to take a leaf from this woman
who spoke of the mass of blood-red worms as if it was a rose,
and you fresh in the grave, and I unable to help
picture you, in your coffin dark, covered with such a posy
all the way from your roman nose to your pedicured toes.

THE BIRDS

At dinner a friend admired the regular birds at our feeder:
the seal-sleek grackles, the rouged house finch,
the natty chickadees, the tan mourning doves.
She asks, being a bird lover, if we'd unusual ones of late.
I mentioned the cowbirds of today. She made a face,
explained to the company how the cowbird is worse
than any Old World cuckoo, lays eggs in a wider range
of foster nests; the cowfledgling kills the usurped brood.
As others at the table grimaced, I admitted a fondness
for the cowbird, this cowboy in the brown hood,
who, according to bird-heads, are thus since following
bison across the plains, without any time to nest.
What else could these creatures do? We survive rightly
or wrongly. And who are we to talk, us American flock?
The birds might ask—even the cowbird—who is
any person to talk? Where are the great bison herds now?
Ah, don't be so hard on the cowbirds.
They're simply caught up in old ways. And, besides,
I like their silly finch-beaks stuck on their crow heads
like those characters in that Greek comedy
about a better world, with bird beaks stuck on their pates.
Yes, like one of those characters in a Greek comedy.

THE SKUNK MOTHS

The family of skunks, their backs to me from our deck,
      are like great black-and-white caterpillars. I imagine them
the giant larvae of luna moths or monarch butterflies,
      their pupae unzipping, tremendous wings unfolding,
fluttering about the summer airways, big as people;
      each revanchist proboscis exacting retribution for those
we've not let flutter down the summers. Imagine
      their eyes, big as cow eyes, gazing, gazing at us.
Imagine the luna's gossamer tulle wings, the tippets
      brushing us, fanning us tenderly, wrapping us in a veil,
bringing us gently to our knees in a gathering humility,
      brushing aside our mortification, finally at home, natural
in the natural world—their wings our cocoon—becoming
ourselves, pinioned resplendence, at last the human mothfly.

Envoi

THE NEW VOYAGER

To Daniel, as I recall your mother having her monitor check during the
2000 presidential election and the monitor picking up a local radio.

It was uncanny that morning how the Doppler,
       flying-saucered across the globe of your mother,
picked up our future commander and chief promising a golden world,
       his voice coming through like a scratched record—you curled
          in your womb-whirligig, our terrestrial.
Shades of Voyager's gold record to be played by extraterrestrials
       light years away, spinning with the world's salutary
          lingoes, music, flora and fauna—some already history—
without mention of war-making; the needless extra terrestrial
       lacrimae rerum; or the excluded photograph of a couple
          strolling naked, the woman expecting,
vetoed not because they're the spitting image of the starving
       myriads (each belly-bloated with nothing),
          but in blushing shame of the body.
Now that you've disembarked your mum module,
       I close with this, not without apology,
          and launch this ephemerally sealed capsule.